ABUNDANT TRUTH INTERNATIONAL MINISTRIES

Apostolic Ministry Revival Series

THE APOSTOLIC REVOLUTION

Exploring the Apostolic Restoration and Reformation

Roderick Levi Evans

The Apostolic Revolution

Exploring the Apostolic Restoration and Reformation

All Rights Reserved ©2011 by Roderick L. Evans

No part of this book may be reproduced or transmitted in any form or by any means, graphic, electronic, or mechanical, including photocopying, recording, taping, or by any information storage or retrieval system, without the permission in writing from the publisher.

Front & Back Cover Designs by
Abundant Truth Publishing, U.S.A. All rights reserved.

Abundant Truth Publishing
an imprint of Abundant Truth International Ministries

For information address:
Abundant Truth International
P.O. Box 126
Camden, NC 27921

ISBN 13: 9781601411044

Printed in the United States of America

Unless otherwise indicated, all of the scripture quotations are taken from the Authorized King James Version of the Bible. Scripture quotations marked with NIV are taken from the New International Version of the Bible. Scripture quotations marked with NASV are taken from the New American Standard Version of the Bible. Scripture quotations marked with Amplified are taken from the Amplified Bible.

Contents

Preface
Introduction

Chapter 1 – The Apostolic Restoration   1

The Ancestral Demonstrations   3

The Apostolic Restored   9

Chapter 2 - The Apostolic Representative   15

Obedience   17

Faithfulness   19

Love   22

Authentic Apostolic Ministry   26

Chapter 3 - The Apostolic Refused   33

Judas' Beliefs   37

Contents (cont.)

Judas' Betrayal   42

Chapter 4 - The Apostolic Rejected   55

Judas' Bleak End   57

The Case for Rejection   63

Chapter 5 - The Apostolic Respected   69

Peter's Insight   73

Peter's Integrity   75

Peter's Invocation   79

Preface

Apostles and apostolic ministry are important to the furtherance of the Kingdom of God and the Church. It is my prayer that the information presented in this work will prepare believers for the reformation that will occur in the demonstration of the apostolic ministry.

Numerous works have been produced which highlight the ministry of the apostle. However, the information in this book will bring believers into a greater understanding of the shift coming to apostles and apostolic ministry.

Roderick Levi Evans

Introduction

As the disciples waited for the promise of the Faithe; that is, the baptism of the Holy Ghost, they cast lots to discover who would replace Judas. When the qualified candidate was selected, they continued in prayer.

After this, the Holy Spirit came upon those gathered in the upper room, and they instantly became powerful witnesses of the Resurrection. Souls were converted and the new converts were confirmed in the faith. The Apostolic Ministry Revival

Series was developed to reveal how God is bringing a restoration and revival to apostles and apostolic ministry for an end time expansion of the Kingdom of God and establishing of believers in the faith.

In this publication:

Controversy over the gifts and ministries of the Spirit has abounded for centuries. Various scholars have taught that there was a cessation of the gifts and ministries. More specifically, they affirm that the ministry of the Apostle is no longer in operation nor valid. However, in recent years, a resurgence of the operation and demonstration of this ministry occurred.

Traditional and Non-traditional churches, alike, have experienced the visitation of God through the Holy Spirit.

Since the emergence and acceptance of the ministries and gifts of the Holy Spirit, various authors have written concerning this phenomenon.

In spite of this, many in the Church, presently, do not understand the functions and operations of, namely, the office of the Apostle. Even in organizations and denominations that consider this ministry valid today, comprehension is oftentimes elementary.

Where there is no clear understanding, individuals become vulnerable to deception and error. Many apostles have abused their ministries and authority. Therefore, the Lord is going to send a reformation in the midst of the Church. It is designed to bring purity again to the apostolic office. Not only in the execution of this ministry, but also in the perspective for which it is received.

In the first book of this series, we will show the events that led to the primary apostolic revolution in the early Church. We will discuss how there was a need for a replacement in the early apostles which was the prerequisite for the outpouring of the Spirit and formation and foundation of the establishment of the New Testament faith and early disciples.

THE APOSTOLIC REVOLUTION Exploring the Apostolic Restoration and Reformation

-Chapter 1-

The Apostolic Restoration

THE APOSTOLIC REVOLUTION Exploring the Apostolic Restoration and Reformation

Apostolic Ministry Revival Series 2

"Elias truly shall first come and restore all things (Matthew 17:11)." Jesus' words revealed God's wisdom in restoration. Throughout history, when God wanted restoration of fellowship with man, He would send an individual to prepare the way. God spoke to Noah to warn of His impending destruction of the world. No man heard him and only he and his family were saved.

The Ancestral Demonstrations

After man multiplied upon the face of the earth, God chose Abraham to be the Father of many nations through faith in Him. At the appointed time of Israel's exodus from Egypt, God sent Moses as the deliverer and giver of the Law. All of these men were used to restore the proper worship of God.

Israel's history reflects God's desire for continual fellowship with mankind. However, when they broke covenant and fellowship, God used the prophets to call for repentance and restoration. One of the most notable prophets of Jewish history is Elijah (Elias, in some translations).

When Israel (through Ahab and Jezebel's evil reign) strayed away from the

Lord, God sent Elijah to challenge the wickedness and restore Israel to God. His words on Mount Carmel reveal his mission.

> *And Elijah came unto all the people, and said, How long halt ye between two opinions? If the Lord be God, follow him: but if Baal, then follow him. And the people answered him not a word. (I Kings 18:21)*

Because of the character and power demonstrated in Elijah's ministry, he became the symbol of repentance and restoration Malachi revealed this truth in his prophetic messages.

> *Behold, I will send you Elijah the prophet before the coming of the great and dreadful day of the Lord. And he shall turn the heart of the fathers to the children, and the heart of the children to their fathers, lest I come and smite the earth with a curse. (Malachi 4:5-6)*

Before the Messiah came, Malachi revealed that Elijah would come first. His job was to restore fathers and children. Spiritually, he would turn the hearts of men unto God. We discover that God did not send the first Elijah back, but He sent a man who came in the spirit and likeness of Elijah; that is, John, the Baptist.

> *In those days came John the Baptist, preaching in the wilderness of Judaea, And saying, Repent ye: for the kingdom of heaven is at hand. (Matthew 3:1-2)*

In his time, John was a modern day 'Elijah' challenging the established religious system of the day. His mission was to bring restoration. He restored man's perspective and worship of God through baptism unto repentance. This, in turn, prepared man for the One who was to come.

When He came, the fullness of the Father and His purposes would be revealed. We see demonstrated in Abraham, Elijah, and John ancestral demonstrations of apostolic ministry.

Today, we find that God is bringing a full restoration of the ministries and gifts of the Spirit in the Church. In recent decades, the prophetic ministry became very prominent. Like Elijah, today's true prophets challenged the hypocrisy and covetousness of this generation.

John (in Elijah's spirit) prepared the world for the Apostle of the Faith. Thus, the prophetic ministry corporately functioned as the "Elijah," which was to come, preparing the way for the apostles.

And Jesus answered and said unto them, Elias truly shall first come, and restore all things. (Matthew 17:11)

The Apostolic Restored

The apostolic paradigm shift begins with a restoration. In recent years, three dimensions of the apostolic have been restored. The first is the sending forth and the acceptance of modern-day apostles. God released individuals into the Kingdom of God who without a doubt could be classified as apostles. Again, the corporate ministry of the prophets prepared the way.

The second is the work of the modern-day apostles. The apostles that came forth restored understanding of the apostolic office, ministry, and function.

Without this, immature and false apostles would continue to damage the credibility of those who are mature and true; subsequently, frustrating God's plan for the apostolic ministry presently.

The third dimension of the apostolic restoration is the required character of apostles. This results in a restoration of appreciation and respect for apostles and their ministries. It is within this third area of restoration that we discover the heart of the apostolic paradigm shift.

The paradigm shift will not only take place in the acceptance and work of apostles, but in the character reflected in those in this ministry. Jesus is called the Apostle and High Priest of the Faith.

Wherefore, holy brethren, partakers of the heavenly calling, consider the Apostle and High Priest of our profession, Christ Jesus. (Hebrews 3:6)

He set the standard for apostles and apostolic ministry. When we understand how he functioned as an apostle, we can discover why an apostolic paradigm shift is necessary. Jesus is the true apostolic representative.

Notes:

THE APOSTOLIC REVOLUTION
Exploring the Apostolic Restoration and Reformation

-Chapter 2-

The Apostolic Representative

The apostolic reformation comes to produce apostles who will mirror the apostolic ministry of the Christ. The standard set by Christ went beyond fulfilling God's plan. He showed us that we were to fulfill His plan with character. Three things characterized Jesus' apostolic ministry and character.

Obedience

As the Apostle, Jesus walked in obedience to the Father. He was not self-willed or stubborn. He did not rebel against the commission given to Him. Hebrews declared Jesus' understanding of

His ministry.

> *Then said I, Lo, I come (in the volume of the book it is written of me,) to do thy will, O God. (Hebrews 10:7)*

Jesus came only to do the will of God. He did not have any other agenda. His ministry exhibited total obedience to God. Hear the words of His testimony,

> *For I came down from heaven, not to do mine own will, but the will of him that sent me. (John 6:38)*

If obedience is not the foundation of the apostle's ministry, it will be defective and ineffective. If Jesus walked in obedience to the Father and He was Lord of all, the apostle has to have the same mind. Jesus' obedience included His ministry and lifestyle. He was blameless and without sin.

The apostle's obedience has to reflect this. After preaching, teaching, prophesying, evangelizing, and ministering, the apostle has to walk in obedience to God's standards for holy and righteous living, which involves personality traits also.

Faithfulness

As the apostolic representative,

Jesus demonstrated the faithfulness required in an apostle. After revealing Christ as the Apostle of the Faith, the writer of Hebrews revealed His faithfulness.

> *...consider the Apostle and High Priest of our profession, Christ Jesus; who was faithful to him that appointed him, as also Moses was faithful in all his house. (Hebrews 3:1b - 2)*

Jesus added faithfulness to obedience. He did not quit or shun His responsibilities because of adversity. He tolerated endless criticism and rejection. He also endured the pain and agony of the cross. He did not allow His trials, test, and troubles to hinder Him.

Every apostle has to remain faithful to the calling. The apostolic ministry brings controversy and contention. Faithfulness sustains the apostle in times of struggle.

Jesus remained faithful to the Father. The modern-day apostle has to remain faithful in spite of consistent rejection, and misunderstanding. Apostles today should reflect the faithfulness of Christ.

Love

Jesus' obedience and faithfulness in His earthly ministry was tempered by love. Christ's motivation in ministry was love. He remained obedient and faithful because He loved God and He loved mankind. He fulfilled the greatest of the commandments.

Master, which is the great commandment in the law? Jesus said unto him, Thou shalt love the Lord thy God with all thy heart, and with all thy soul, and with all thy mind. This is the first and great commandment. And the second is like unto it, Thou shalt love thy neighbour as thyself. (Matthew 22:36-39)

Because of love, Jesus remained focused on His mission. The modern-day apostle's foundation for ministry has to be love. In my book, *The Apostle Question (pgs. 55-56)*, the character traits of the apostle revealed through love were examined. Love governed Christ's actions and it has to rule in the apostolic minister today. Here is the excerpt,

"Love has to be the foundation of the

apostle's ministry. God is love. Christ demonstrated His love for us through His obedience to God and His death on the cross.

God's involvement with men is always through His love. His correction and discipline is rooted in love. The apostle has to be the express image of God. No matter what his ministry entails, it must be done through love.

Charity suffereth long, and is kind; charity envieth not; charity vaunteth not itself, is not puffed up, doth not behave itself unseemly, seeketh not her own, is not easily provoked, thinketh no evil; rejoiceth not in iniquity, but rejoiceth in the truth; Beareth all things, believeth all things, hopeth all things, and endureth all things. (I Corinthians 13:4-7)

The apostle has to have an everlasting love for God, the Church, and his family. If he rebukes, corrects, admonishes, teaches, warns, and prays, love has to be the source. The apostle's demonstration of love must *match Paul's description of love as recorded in I Corinthians 13."*

Jesus is the true apostolic representative. His life and ministry stands as the model of valid apostolic ministry. If apostles today possess the obedience, faithfulness, and love of Christ, they will become effective vessels in the present-day reformation.

Authentic Apostolic Ministry

When authentic apostles and apostolic ministry function properly, God's plan and purpose for the Church will be realized. The apostolic restoration, reformation, and ensuing paradigm shift finds its definition within the biblical account of the disciples in the upper room.

After Jesus' ascension, the disciples waited for the outpouring of the Holy Spirit. The events in the upper room before Pentecost clearly demonstrate the totality of the apostolic reformation and paradigm shift presently taking place (Acts 1:15-26).

While in the upper room, we can identify four apostolic personalities. Understanding of these will clarify the apostolic paradigm shift of today.

The first two will be discussed in this book, and the following book of this series.

Judas – The Apostolic Rejected

> *For it is written in the book of Psalms, Let his habitation be desolate, and let no man dwell therein: and his bishoprick let another take. (Acts 1:20)*

Peter – The Apostolic Respected

> *And in those days Peter stood up in the midst of the disciples... (Acts1: 15)*

Matthias – The Apostolic Paradigm shift

> *And they gave forth their lots; and the lot fell upon Matthias; and he was numbered with the eleven apostles. (Acts 1:26)*

Joseph – The Apostolic Representation

> *And they appointed two, Joseph called Barsabas, who was surnamed Justus, and Matthias. (Acts 1:23)*

The manifestation of these apostolic personalities produced a reformation of the worship of God and the expansion of the Kingdom of God.

The present-day apostolic reformation

will do the same. The failure of Judas as one of the apostles of the Lamb set the stage for the apostolic reformation of his day. When we understand the apostolic that is rejected, we can embrace the paradigm shift and reformation that is coming.

Notes:

THE APOSTOLIC REVOLUTION
Exploring the Apostolic Restoration and Reformation

-Chapter 3-

The Apostolic Refused

Though Jesus is the perfect representative of apostolic ministry, there is an individual who embodies the refused apostolic ministry; that is, Judas Iscariot. Jesus chose him as an apostle and disciple. The Gospels record,

> *And when it was day, he called unto him his disciples: and of them he chose twelve, whom also he named apostles; Simon, (whom he also named Peter,) and Andrew his brother, James and John, Philip and Bartholomew, Matthew and Thomas, James the son of Alphaeus,*

and Simon called Zelotes, And Judas the brother of James, and Judas Iscariot... (Luke 6:13-16)

Judas had a valid calling accompanied with the power of God. He received power along with the other disciples for ministry.

And when he had called unto him his twelve disciples, he gave them power against unclean spirits, to cast them out, and to heal all manner of sickness and all manner of disease. (Matthew 10:1)

However, Judas rejected his calling

and position; his apostleship was revoked. Through consideration of Judas' beliefs, betrayal, and bleak end, we can identify the apostolic that God has **refused** today.

Judas' Beliefs

What led to Judas' betrayal? The scriptures are unclear as to the exact reason. However, whatever governed Judas' belief system contributed to his betrayal of Christ.

There are numerous theories suggested to explain his treachery. Three are commonly argued: religious fervor, personal greed, and demonic deception.

Religious Fervor

The first theory suggested for Judas' betrayal is religious fervor. Some historians suggest that Judas was a member of a radical Jewish sect called the Zealots. This sect desired to see the Jewish people freed from Roman control.

They dreamt of a day when Israel would be returned to the glory and power that it once possessed. However, the Zealots had a "by any means necessary" attitude. They promoted a violent, physical overthrow of the Roman government.

Since Jesus did not come to release them from Roman control but the control of sin, some propose that Judas betrayed Him because He did not help to support the cause.

It is believed that Judas saw Jesus as a traitor to His people because His zeal to overthrow Rome did not match that of the Zealot sect. Consequently, he sold him to the Pharisees.

Religious Fervor Today

As apostles surface, there are some who fit into this category. They forget that they are ambassadors for Christ and begin to follow their own agendas. Numerous apostles have become concerned with the organization of the Church and the institution of larger buildings, institutions, and community services, while neglecting the advancement of the Kingdom of God, which can only be done through the conversion of souls.

There are apostles today who are on the road to betraying Christ because they became consumed with the work of the Lord and left Him out. Other apostles become ambassadors for the apostolic ministry rather than Christ.

They began to preach that apostles are the cornerstone of the Church rather than Christ. They become so consumed with trying to establish the role of apostolic ministry in the Church that they forget to demonstrate it. They began to preach apostles and not Christ.

Whenever religious activities and ministries become the central focus of an apostle, they become spiritual Zealots for the wrong cause. If Judas was a Zealot, his personal agenda caused him to betray Christ for his own cause.

Judas' Betrayal

Apostles today are experiencing refusal from the Father because they are working for their advancement and not the Kingdom of God.

Personal Greed

The second commonly proposed theory is that Judas was greedy. It has also been suggested that Judas became disillusioned with Christ because it did not lead him into personal wealth. Before Jesus called Judas, it is reported that he was a thief. However, in service to the Lord, he was responsible for the finances.

This he said (Judas), not that he cared for the poor; but because he was a thief, and had the bag, and bare what was put therein. (John 12:6, Parenthesis mine)

From this, it is argued that Judas expected the fame of Christ to bring him fortune. From the scriptures, we understand that Christ did not live as a king, but He lived modestly (oftentimes depending on the hospitality of others) in ministry. Judas, again, may have been disappointed and saw Jesus' betrayal as a way to make some money.

Personal Greed Today

Numerous ministers, especially apostles are candidates for refusal because of personal greed. The apostolic that is refused is one that values money over ministry. There are apostles whose apostleship will be or has been revoked because of greed. They use their God-given authority and position to get wealthy. They use clichés to get money from the Lord's people.

Judas was greedy. His greed was not under control though he walked with Jesus. This is why he had a problem with the woman anointing Jesus' feet with oil. He wanted to get the money in his possession. It is believed that this act pushed him over the edge. The gospels record that immediately following this incident that he conspired to betray Him.

> *She hath done what she could: she is come aforehand to anoint my body to the burying. Verily I say unto you, Wheresoever this gospel shall be preached throughout the whole world, this also that she hath done shall be spoken of for a memorial of*

her. And Judas Iscariot, one of the twelve, went unto the chief priests, to betray him unto them. And when they heard it, they were glad, and promised to give him money. And he sought how he might conveniently betray him. (Mark 14:8-11)

Apostles who are candidates for refusal deter others from giving to please Christ to giving to only 'bless' the apostle of God. Judas was refused and apostles today will face refusal. Greed will definitely lead to betrayal.

Demonic Deception

The third theory is that Judas submitted to demonically induced deception. His suspected religious fervor and personal greed had little impact on his betrayal. Support for this comes from scriptures also,

> *And supper being ended, the devil having now put into the heart of Judas Iscariot, Simon's son, to betray him. (John 13:2)*

The scriptures are clear that Judas' betrayal was strengthened by demonic influence. He had previously discussed arrangements with the Pharisees for Jesus' betrayal, but the devil made sure that he went through with it.

This demonstrates that the adversary capitalized on the wickedness already present within Judas. This gave him no defense against demonic influence.

Demonic Deception Today

Judas allowed the devil to deceive him into betrayal. Though he walked with Jesus, he did not allow His teachings to change his heart though he participated in His work.

...lest that by any means, when I

have preached to others, I myself should be a castaway. (I Corinthians 9:27b)

There are apostles today who operate in ministry with success. Yet, they have not allowed the ministry they have preached to change them inwardly. They leave themselves open to demonic influence.

Apostles who are self-willed, stubborn, arrogant, and prideful are subject to demonic delusion. In this state, they become candidates for refusal.

Regardless of one's personal opinion concerning Judas' beliefs, it is clear that any apostles who hold to them will be or have been refused of God. Judas serves as a warning to all: Do not allow ungodly belief systems to govern ministerial activities! Judas' betrayal was solidified with a kiss.

Apostles have to guard against blessing Christ with their mouths and betraying them with their activities. Revocation of apostleship will be inevitable. Judas did not enjoy the money that he received for the betrayal. Those who lose their apostleship will discover that the reward addressed this truth in this manner,

> *For many walk, of whom I have told you often, and now tell you even weeping, that they are the enemies of the cross of Christ. (Philippians 3:18-19)*

Notes:

THE APOSTOLIC REVOLUTION
Exploring the Apostolic Restoration and Reformation

-Chapter 4-

The Apostolic Rejected

THE APOSTOLIC REVOLUTION Exploring the Apostolic Restoration and Reformation

Rejected apostles will experience shame and sorrow as God fills their positions with faithful servants.

Judas' Bleak End

Judas' betrayal of Christ did not end with his restoration. His story concluded with suicide. Judas' demise is recalled in complimenting accounts of his last moments.

> *And he cast down the pieces of silver in the temple, and departed, and went and hanged himself. (Matthew 27:5)*
>
> *Now this man purchased a field with*

> *the reward of iniquity; and falling headlong, he burst asunder in the midst, and all his bowels gushed out. (Acts 1:18)*

Judas ended his own life. Rejected apostles, likewise, commit spiritual suicide. Peter's corresponding account of what happened to Judas reveals what happens to an apostle on the road to rejection. All can recognize these traits. Three things occurred in Judas' end.

Purchased a Field with the Reward of Iniquity

Rejected apostles and apostolic

ministers engage in ungodly practices for personal gain. The betrayal money Judas received was used to purchase a field. Rejected apostolic ministries will acquire positions, authority, wealth, promotions, and favor through the exercise of ungodly character traits.

Be mindful of apostles and apostolic individuals who equate godliness with gain. This mindset is popular among those who are on the way to rejection.

> *Perverse disputings of men of corrupt minds, and destitute of the truth, supposing that gain is*

godliness: from such withdraw thyself. (I Timothy 6:5)

Though God delights in the prosperity of His saints, any apostles whose message focuses solely on this truth set themselves up for a fall.

Fell Headlong

After hanging himself, Judas fell headlong to the ground. In other words, he fell headfirst. Falling headlong represents apostles who become heady and high-minded; that is, prideful. Pride has subdued countless ministries throughout the ages. To help Paul resist pride, God gave him a thorn in the flesh.

Apostles on the path to rejection are full of pride. They, like Judas, fall headfirst. The scriptures declare that pride paves the way for destruction.

Pride goeth before destruction, and an haughty spirit before a fall. (Proverbs 16: 18)

Beware of apostles and apostolic individuals who promote themselves and their ministries only. Their ministries consist of comparing themselves with others and exalting their personal accomplishments. Their sermons consist of testimonies of their greatness rather than the declaration of His greatness. Rejected apostles subject themselves to the same fate as Judas and will fall headfirst as he did.

He burst Asunder & Bowels Gushed Out

Judas fell headfirst. Yet, when he hit the ground, his stomach was split in two. Consequently, his intestines (bowels) spilled out. Rejected apostles depart from following God to pursuing the lusts of the flesh. In the scriptures, those who became false made a god out of their bellies.

Whose end is destruction, whose God is their belly, and whose glory is in their shame, who mind earthly things. (Philippians 3:19)

Rejected apostles will be disciplined and judged according to their evil desires. The bowels spilling represents God exposing those whom he has rejected. The hidden desires and motives will be revealed to all.

The Case for Rejection

Some reading this will think that God will not revoke an individual's ministry. There is precedent for such an act in the scriptures.

If God does not change and Christ is the same yesterday, today, and forever, we can safely conclude that continual rebellion in the New Covenant Church will result in revocation of ministry. King Saul rebelled and refused to follow the Lord repeatedly. God rejected him.

For rebellion is as the sin of witchcraft, and stubbornness is as iniquity and idolatry. Because thou hast rejected the word of the Lord, he hath also rejected thee from being king. (I Samuel 15:23)

He revoked the kingdom from him and his seed. In spite of this, Samuel continued to pray for him. However, God did not receive his prayer for the rebellious and self-willed king.

> *And the Lord said unto Samuel, How long wilt thou mourn for Saul, seeing I have rejected him from reigning over Israel? (I Samuel 16:1a)*

King Saul's persistent rebellion and refusal to follow the Lord wholeheartedly resulted in God's rejection of him. Saul was king without the presence and endorsement of the Lord. Though he continued to reign for some years, he was still rejected.

There are apostolic ministers, today, who are rejected but allowed to maintain their positions. Like Saul, God no longer endorses them. Rather than repent, they are satisfied to keep a title and position. If continual rebellion resulted in Saul's rejection, continual rebellion will result in an apostle's rejection.

Notes:

-Chapter 5-

The Apostolic Respected

Because many apostles have subjected themselves to the pursuit of this world's goods, fortune, and fame, they have walked in the way of Judas, the rejected apostle. They have contributed to the increase of the rejected apostolic. In turn, God is sending forth apostles in these days who will walk in the obedience, faithfulness, and love of Christ.

The apostolic reformation will be ushered in with the assistance of established apostolic ministers. In the upper room, Peter recognized Judas' rejection and the need for a replacement.

And in those days Peter stood up in the midst of the disciples, and said, (the number of names together were about an hundred and twenty,) Men and brethren, this scripture must needs have been fulfilled, which the Holy Ghost by the mouth of David spake before concerning Judas, which was guide to them that took Jesus. (Acts 1:15-16)

In order for the reformation to come into fruition, established apostles are responsible to bring forward the new company of apostles God is sending forth.

Peter represents the apostolic that is respected. He recognized that there was someone else needed to stand with them in ministry as apostles of the Lamb. Apostles who want to take part in what God is doing have to follow in Peter's example.

Peter's Insight

In the upper room, the disciples gathered to wait upon the reception of the Holy Ghost. It was in this atmosphere that Peter demonstrated insight into the purposes of God. He understood that Judas' actions fulfilled prophecy. And again, there was a need to fill his position based upon that which was revealed in the scriptures.

Peter exhibited apostolic insight. He was knowledgeable of the scriptures and he knew how to apply them to the present situation. Because of this, he became the catalyst for the restoration and reformation of the apostolic ministry originally purposed by Christ, which consisted of twelve apostles.

Apostolic Insight Today

Apostles today need spiritual insight into the upcoming move of God. Like

Peter, they need to understand the scriptures and their impact on what is occurring today. Mature apostles will see the need for true apostolic ministers and assist in their entrance into kingdom work.

Peter's Integrity

Along with spiritual insight, Peter displayed integrity. Judas' rejection left a vacancy that needed to be filled. Peter did not try to reserve a special place for himself and the other apostles.

He demonstrated selflessness in apostolic ministry. He wanted others whom the Lord had chosen to come forward in ministry. He was concerned with the work of the kingdom and not personal glory. In response to this, he put forth an inquiry to the other disciples. He wanted to find someone who would be able to replace Judas.

> *For it is written in the book of Psalms, Let his habitation be desolate, and let no man dwell therein: and his bishoprick let another take. Wherefore of thes men which have companied with us all the time that the Lord Jesus went in and out among us? (Acts 1:20-21)*

Apostolic Integrity Today

Apostles today have to walk in the integrity of Peter. Some apostles feel that they are the only true apostles left and feel that no one else can stand with them in ministry. This was not Peter's view.

He knew that in order for the work to be accomplished, others were needed to help. Apostles today need this mindset. Apostles have the responsibility to facilitate new ministries into the Body.

But Barnabas took him, and brought him to the apostles, and declared unto them how he had seen the Lord in the way, and that he had spoken to him, and how he had preached boldly at Damascus in the name of Jesus. (Acts 9:27)

Today's established apostles have to do for apostolic ministers what Barnabas did for Paul. Since there was controversy surrounding Paul's conversion, Barnabas (a respected disciple) presented him to the Church.

Apostles have to guard against trying to protect a position or title and allow God to use them to accomplish His purposes.

Peter's Invocation

Following Peter's insight, integrity, and inquiry concerning the need for the rejected apostle's replacement, he and the disciples prayed. They prayed for God to reveal *His* choice.

And they prayed, and said, Thou, Lord, which knowest the hearts of all men, shew whether of these two thou hast chosen, That he may take part of this ministry and apostleship... (Acts 1:24-25a)

Peter's insight produced action. They prayed until God gave revelation of Judas' replacement. He and the others knew that the one chosen to stand with them needed to have God's endorsement. Though they look for suitable candidates, the Lord gave the final endorsement.

Apostolic Invocation Today

The respected apostolic of today and the established apostles have to give themselves to prayer to effectuate the apostolic reformation that is occurring. Peter's revelation led to invocation. Those apostles who have understanding of the apostolic transition have to be willing to labor in intercessory prayer until those whom God has chosen, take their rightful positions.

Because Peter recognized the vacancy and was a catalyst for filling the void, it led to a paradigm shift in apostolic ministry and in the Church. The same, which, is happening today.

In the next book, we will explore the events in the upper room, the outpouring of the Sprit, and the first apostolic revolution, which sets the precedence for the apostolic paradigm shift occurring presently.

Notes:

THE APOSTOLIC REVOLUTION
Exploring the Apostolic Restoration and Reformation

www.ingramcontent.com/pod-product-compliance
Lightning Source LLC
Chambersburg PA
CBHW072013030526
44119CB00064B/674